# THE
# MEDIEVAL
# WOMAN

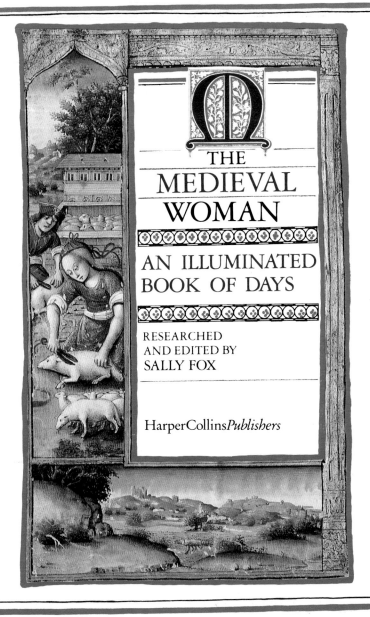

# THE
# MEDIEVAL
# WOMAN

## AN ILLUMINATED
## BOOK OF DAYS

RESEARCHED
AND EDITED BY
SALLY FOX

HarperCollins*Publishers*

# DEDICATION

This book is dedicated to my mother, who showed me there is no end to a woman's growth, and to my husband and sons who grew with me.

Cover illustration:
HARVESTING FRUIT. October (detail)
*Heures de la Duchesse de Bourgogne.* MS. 76/1362, f. 10v.
French, c. 1450
Musée Condé, Chantilly (Ph: Lauros-Giraudon/Art Resource)

Title page illustration:
SHEARING SHEEP. June (detail)
*Petites Heures d'Anne de Bretagne.* MS. Lat. n.a. 3027, f. 3v.
French, beginning sixteenth century
Bibliothèque Nationale, Paris

HarperCollins*Publishers*
77–85 Fulham Palace Road,
Hammersmith, London W6 8JB

Published by HarperCollins*Publishers* 1993
9 8 7 6 5 4 3 2 1

First published in Great Britain by Collins 1990
Reprinted six times

Copyright © Sally Fox 1985

A catalogue record for this book is
available from the British Library

ISBN 0 00 217514 2

Printed in Spain

D.L.TO:45-1993

# ACKNOWLEDGEMENTS

The author is grateful to Mira Van Doren, whose inspired suggestion led to this research; and to Dr. Pamela Berger of Boston College and Roger Wieck of Tufts University for their generous advice. The staffs of the following institutions gave sympathetic assistance: Beinecke Rare Book and Manuscript Library, Yale University, New Haven; Bibliothèque Sainte-Geneviève, Paris; Bibliothèque Nationale, Paris; Bodleian Library, Oxford; The British Library, London; Centre Medico-Technique de l'Assistance Publique, Paris; Christ Church Library, Oxford; The Historical Library, Yale Medical School, New Haven; The Houghton Library, Harvard University, Cambridge, Mass.; Massachusetts College of Pharmacy, Boston; The Metropolitan Museum of Art, New York; The Museum of Fine Arts, Boston; The Pierpont Morgan Library, New York; The Rare Book and Manuscript Room, Boston Public Library; The Rare Book Room, Countway Library, Harvard Medical School, Boston; The Rare Book and Manuscript Division, New York Public Library; The Walters Art Gallery, Baltimore.

In addition, the author also would like to take this opportunity to thank the staff of Bulfinch Press. The publication of this pictorial Book of Days acknowledges the profession of picture research, which, although a greatly respected profession in Europe, often remains unrecognized in the United States.

# THE MEDIEVAL WOMAN AT WORK

To study history is constantly to rediscover the past. Until recently conventional history concentrated on sources focusing on men in power and the consequences of their power. Historians today are uncovering other primary sources, documents and artifacts of past societies that make it possible to better understand and complete our picture of those societies and to re-create the daily lives of ordinary people. Because most histories have been written by men, the role of women has usually been ignored or taken for granted. As a result, more than half the population has been historically invisible. The illuminations in this book come from manuscripts produced primarily in the years 1300 to 1550. By showing us the many and varied occupations of women in the later Middle Ages, these illuminations restore some of the lost history of women. Real medieval women were quite different from the image of women portrayed by the Church or by the romantic literature that was popular with the aristocracy of the time. In the teachings of the Church, women were either worshipped like the virtuous Virgin Mary, or subjected and scorned like the sinful and inferior Eve. In the age of chivalry, adoration of the lady was the worldly counterpart of the cult of the Virgin, but the romantic precepts of courtly love affected only a small segment of the upper classes. Even there, this adoration may have had little meaning, since wife beating was allowed by canon law. How can we get beyond the images created by the Church and popular romances to discover the real world of medieval women? Letters, wills, business and legal documents, convent, manor and census records all help. But manuscript illuminations and woodcuts from the first printed books can also be used as documents to complete our picture of their world. The years 1300 to 1550 were years of transition between the breakdown of the feudal system and the beginnings of modern Europe. The main development of the time was the rise of the commercial middle class, with an economy based on money rather than land. As towns and cities grew, power gradually shifted from the landed nobles and the Church to the developing middle class. Along with the growing secularization of European society came greater use of the vernacular in literature, further spurred by the invention of the printing press. Some laywomen influenced these developments by acquiring libraries, producing books and paying for translations from the Latin. It is probably because of this secularization that illustrations, both illuminations and woodcuts, began to depict more of the actual world. To know what a woman's life was like in that period, we first need to know her place in society. Was she a noblewoman, a peasant, or a bourgeoise? In all classes women were subject to expectations specific to their class. At the same time, the records show, as do these illuminations, that women often undertook the same tasks as the men in their class. Far from the common image of pampered creatures, the ladies of the manor were well-trained and responsible managers who ran complicated estates. Because their husbands were often absent, fighting in the Crusades or other battles, responsibility for the ongoing life of the fiefs fell on female shoulders. Each estate had to be as nearly self-sufficient as possible. Women had to manage large tracts of land, apply principles of agriculture and animal husbandry, manage hundreds of farmers and servants and their families, settle disputes, supervise the preparation and storage of foods and goods made on the estate, have a practical knowledge of medicine, and even defend the castle and estate when attacked, an occurrence particularly likely when neighboring lords knew the manor lady was alone. Clearly, the life of a manor lady was not one of idleness. Peasant women undertook all the traditional farming tasks, including running the dairy, brewing the ale, spinning and weaving, even heavy plowing when necessary. Like farm women everywhere, they had a hard life. If they were widows, they were expected to run the farm and, as before, continue to pay a share of the produce to the lord, as well as to care for their families. In the growing middle class, women often practiced skilled trades usually considered men's work, working as apothecaries, barbers, artists, silkworkers, armorers, tailors and in other trades requiring apprenticeship. Although most guilds officially excluded women, exceptions were made for the trained wives and daughters of guildsmen. It was, after all, necessary to have someone experienced to mind the shop, train the apprentices and carry on the business when the men of the family were traveling. Widows also were able to continue their husbands' businesses. Some women were considered *femmes soles,* a legal term that meant independent women traders. They included not only widows and single women, but also married women who, in some cases, bore sole financial responsibility for their businesses. Some skills were practiced by women of all classes. Many illuminations show women spinning, carding wool and weaving because women *were* the textile industry.

Midwifery was always women's work, and women were expected to deal with everyday medical and surgical emergencies in their own homes. However, if a woman wanted to practice medicine or even undertake simple healing practices outside her home, she ran the risk of social and legal censure; and worst of all, she could be branded a witch. Nevertheless, some women, especially wives and daughters of physicians, were given specific training as doctors, surgeons and nurses. As these illuminations show, women were professional artists who painted frescoes, religious images and portraits, as well as carved bas-reliefs and sculptures. They were professional musicians and troubadours. They wrote and produced books — for instance, Christine de Pisan, considered the first French professional woman writer. Born in 1363, married at fifteen and widowed at twenty-five, she turned to writing verse, allegories and epics to support her three children and mother. Much of her work was written in praise of women of all classes; she defended them against the demeaning image of women presented by that most popular allegorical poem of the Middle Ages, the *Roman de la Rose*. Because the medieval economy was based on land, marriage between members of the upper classes was a business contract drawn to protect and enlarge the inherited holdings. Most women were generally married by fourteen and were expected to provide a dowry. It is interesting that in some areas, women, either single or widowed, could inherit land and make wills. The convents offered an acceptable alternative to marriage. Because dowries were required, nuns usually came from the upper classes and the bourgeoisie. Nunneries often provided the best means of getting an education. They gave women a chance to lead useful lives devoted to running schools and hospitals, managing convent lands and caring for the needy. Single peasant women did not have this option and spent their lives in manual labor. The research and choice of these illuminations were determined by the desire to uncover the work women actually did in the past. Although many of these miniatures were originally intended as illustrations for biblical subjects, scenes from allegories or romances, the illuminators chose to visually describe these stories with women working at occupations clearly familiar to the late medieval artist. One can easily identify with these European women, portrayed more than 500 years ago, as they worked at their daily tasks and professions, either as partners with men, with other women, or by themselves.

L'amour et a la gloire
de la sainte trinite du
pere et du filz et du saint
esperit. Amen. Je comence
a transclater selon mon petit
engier de latin en cler francois
Le livre intitule le lapidaire
A laide du conseil de mes
maistres sur qui ie les ay
entreprins. Si prie a dieu
glorieux quil me donne tele
grace que ie puisse par tele
maniere entendre le sens de
lescripture Que en laide de
mesdits maistres que ad ce
me seront aidans Lesquelz
La benoiste vierge marie ~

voeulle recomander en la pro
tection de son treschier enfant
Ceste emprinse estre mise a ef
fet et a perfection en telle ma
niere que la creature pour qui
ie fais ceste translation le puist
cy entendre si quil sen puist
user a la loenge de la trinite
En laquele guide elle soit a
toute heure recomandee Et
tous ses bien voeullas Amen
Cy fine le prologue.
Cy sensient le lapidaire
selon la verite et loppinion de
ysidore. Ainsi come les pierres
precieuses cy apres escriptes
sont espirituees tant de soie

# JANUARY

|  | 1 |
| --- | --- |
|  | 2 |
|  | 3 |
|  | 4 |
|  | 5 |
|  | 6 |

**SELLING JEWELRY AND SILVER**
Platearius. *Livre des symples medichines, autrement dit Arboriste.*
MS. Fr. 9136, f. 344
French, fifteenth century
Bibliothèque Nationale, Paris

# JANUARY

|  | 7 |
|  | 8 |
|  | 9 |
|  | 10 |
|  | 11 |
|  | 12 |

SPINNING, CARDING, WEAVING
Giovanni Boccaccio. *De claris mulieribus*.
MS. Royal 16 Gv, f. 56
French, fifteenth century
British Library, London

# JANUARY

|  | 13 |
|  | 14 |
|  | 15 |
|  | 16 |
|  | 17 |
|  | 18 |

SELLING BREAD
*Tacuinum Sanitatis*. MS. s.n. 2644, f. 64v
Italian, c. 1385
Österreichische Nationalbibliothek, Vienna

# JANUARY

| | |
|---|---|
| **19** | |
| **20** | |
| **21** | |
| **22** | |
| **23** | |
| **24** | |

SWEEPING
Barthélemy l'Anglais. *Livre des propriétés des choses*.
MS. Fr. 9140, f. 107
French, fifteenth century
Bibliothèque Nationale, Paris

peté peut on q̃ fi dinc des deux ne fot offertes de chofes
tianre de bône Justice e̊ e̊ste. Sensuit listoire de prem

H

san
guere
terra
on mieulx q̃lle fu
ple a escoliere duy
le repute est plꝰ d
il seble surmota
aute de son teps.
lieux son nom for
aucie congnoist
on sit q̃ les brach
artixes tout pꝰ le

paingnt a descript. Ain e celui q̃ ratinas no pas auti
aucais aute. De ceste prene po certau legim fut noble e r
laqlle maistefe aucunemet les argumes a efcriptueme
a demoureret. cestaffi en lufine de la cite vne pucelle

# JANUARY

| | 25 |
|---|---|
| | 26 |
| | 27 |
| | 28 |
| | 29 |
| | 30 |
| | 31 |

ARTIST DESIGNING FRESCO
Giovanni Boccaccio. *Le livre des cleres et nobles femmes.*
MS. Fr. 599, f. 53v
French, fifteenth century
Bibliothèque Nationale, Paris

# FEBRUARY

| 1 |
|---|
| 2 |
| 3 |
| 4 |
| 5 |
| 6 |

SPINNING, CARDING, WEAVING
Giovanni Boccaccio. *Le livre des femmes nobles et renommées*.
MS. Fr. 598, f. 70v
French, fifteenth century
Bibliothèque Nationale, Paris

# FEBRUARY

| | 7 |
| 8 |
| 9 |
| 10 |
| 11 |
| 12 |

WOMAN ENTERTAINER
*Book of Hours.* MS. Rawl. Liturg. E36, f. 90v
French, 1500–1525
Bodleian Library, Oxford

# FEBRUARY

13

14

15

16

17

18

SHOVELING ASHES
Jean Cuba. *Le jardin de santé*. Vol. II. "La cendre"
French, c. 1501
Petit Palais, Paris (Ph: Bulloz)

# FEBRUARY

| | 19 |
| | 20 |
| | 21 |
| | 22 |
| | 23 |
| | 24 |

WOMAN TAILOR CUTTING OUT A PATTERN
Giovanni Boccaccio. *Le livre des cleres et nobles femmes*.
MS. Fr. 599, f. 79v
French, fifteenth century
Bibliothèque Nationale, Paris

# FEBRUARY

| | 25 |
| | 26 |
| | 27 |
| | 28 |
| | 29 |

WOMEN DEFENDING CASTLE WITH BOW
AND CROSSBOW
Walter de Milemete. *De Nobilitatibus, sapientiis, et prudentiis regum.*
MS. CH.CH. 92, f. 4r. English, 1326–7
By kind permission of The Governing Body of Christ Church, Oxford

# MARCH

| | 1 |
| | 2 |
| | 3 |
| | 4 |
| | 5 |
| | 6 |

FAMILY SCENE, WIFE SPINNING WITH DISTAFF
Bourdichon. *Les quatre états de la société. "Le travail"*
French, fifteenth century
École des Beaux-Arts, Paris (Ph: Giraudon/Art Resource)

# MARCH

| | 7 |
| --- | --- |
| | 8 |
| | 9 |
| | 10 |
| | 11 |
| | 12 |

PREPARING AND COOKING TRIPE
*Tacuinum Sanitatis.* MS. s.n. 2644, f. 81r.
Italian, c. 1385
Österreichische Nationalbibliothek, Vienna

# MARCH

| 13 | |
| 14 | |
| 15 | |
| 16 | |
| 17 | |
| 18 | |

NURSE FEEDING SICK MAN (detail)
*Psautier triple de Cantorbery.* MS. Lat. 8846, f. 106
French, fifteenth century
Bibliothèque Nationale, Paris

Apres lenfuit de marie qui
fut de barron bierge perpetuel
le . La . he . bi . Rubriche .

Arie perpetu
elle bierge a
romme ia de
preca de mr
ron li fut :
trounce. tou
te noies de quel barron pas ne

# MARCH

19

20

21

22

23

24

ARTIST PAINTING A SELF-PORTRAIT
Giovanni Boccaccio. *Livre des cleres et nobles femmes*.
MS. Fr. 12420, f. 101v
French, fifteenth century
Bibliothèque Nationale, Paris

# MARCH

| 25 | |
| --- | --- |
| 26 | |
| 27 | |
| 28 | |
| 29 | |
| 30 | |
| 31 | |

PLAYING A HARP
Giovanni Boccaccio. *Le livre des cleres et nobles femmes*.
MS. Fr. 599, f. 68
French, fifteenth century
Bibliothèque Nationale, Paris

**KL** Aprilis habet dies . xxx .
Luna vero . xxix .

| | | |
|---|---|---|
| | g | Theodoræ virginis & mar . |
| xi | A | Mariæ ægyptiacæ |
| | b | Pancratii : mar |
| xix | c | Isidori episcopi |
| viii | d | Vincentii confessoris |
| xvi | e | Cœlestini papæ |
| v | f | Alexandrini mar |
| | g | Dionysii episcopi |
| xiii | A | Prochori : mar . |
| ii | b | Apollonii presb . et mar |

# APRIL

| | 1 |
| | 2 |
| | 3 |
| | 4 |
| | 5 |
| | 6 |

MILKING AND CHURNING BUTTER
*Heures de la Bienheureuse Vierge Marie.* April.
Dutuit B. 37, f. 8r
French, early sixteenth century
Petit Palais, Paris. (Ph: Bulloz)

# APRIL

| | |
|---|---|
| | 7 |
| | 8 |
| | 9 |
| | 10 |
| | 11 |
| | 12 |

SELLING BUTTER
*Tacuinum Sanitatis.* MS. s.n. 2644, f. 61r.
Italian, c. 1385
Österreichische Nationalbibliothek, Vienna

# APRIL

| 13 | |
| 14 | |
| 15 | |
| 16 | |
| 17 | |
| 18 | |

MAKING A NET
Giovanni Boccaccio. *Le livre des cleres et nobles femmes.*
MS. Fr. 599, f. 17v
French, fifteenth century
Bibliothèque Nationale, Paris

Ratue femm
descendant d...
...ple fut fille...
de qui le surnom estoit
turier de lames laquell...
elle ne fust mpe clere p...
Touteffoiz elle estoit a l...
nes oeuvres notables q...
aucune antiens afferm...
ua lusaige de lm a q elle
ua z pourpensa les voi...
prendre les oyseaulx z p...
son fils q auoit nom cho...
ue les fuseaulx couenabl...
de lm estimat et aydant...

rust en son temps maistresse de lart du mestier de tissture z coe la plue...

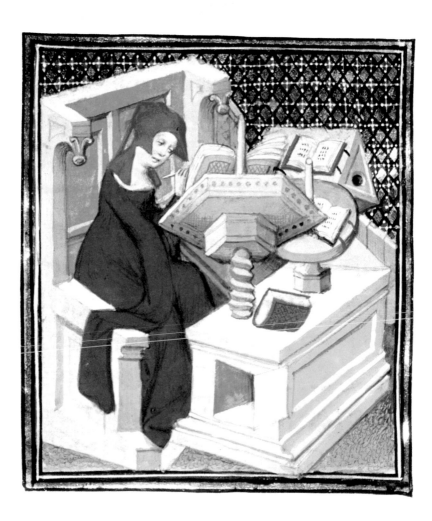

# APRIL

19

20

21

22

23

24

WRITER
Giovanni Boccaccio. *Le livre des femmes nobles et renommées.*
MS. Fr. 598, f. 43r
French, fifteenth century
Bibliothèque Nationale, Paris

Aprilis hab; dies
xxx. luna. xxix.

| | g | |
| xi | | Marie egiptiace |
| xix | b | |
| viij | c | Ambrosij epi. |
| | d | Vincentij conf. |

# APRIL

| | 25 |
|---|---|
| | 26 |
| | 27 |
| | 28 |
| | 29 |
| | 30 |

MANOR LADY SUPERVISING A WOMAN GARDENER
*Book of Hours.* W. 425, f. 4
Flemish, early sixteenth century
The Walters Art Gallery, Baltimore

# MAY

| | 1 |
| | 2 |
| | 3 |
| | 4 |
| | 5 |
| | 6 |

CARRYING A SACK OF WHEAT TO THE MILL
René I, d'Anjou. *Le mortifiement de vaine plaisance.*
MS. 705, f. 38v
French, fifteenth century
The Pierpont Morgan Library, New York

# MAY

<table>
<tr><td>7</td><td></td></tr>
<tr><td>8</td><td></td></tr>
<tr><td>9</td><td></td></tr>
<tr><td>10</td><td></td></tr>
<tr><td>11</td><td></td></tr>
<tr><td>12</td><td></td></tr>
</table>

WOMAN WITH DISTAFF CARRYING A BASKET
OF SPINACH
*Tacuinum Sanitatis.* MS. s.n. 2644, f. 27.
Italian, c. 1385
Österreichische Nationalbibliothek, Vienna

# MAY

| | 13 |
| | 14 |
| | 15 |
| | 16 |
| | 17 |
| | 18 |

DRAWING WATER
Thomas de Cantimpré. *De natura rerum . . . tacuinum sanitatis.* Codex C-67, f. 105r
Italian School, early fifteenth century
Biblioteca Universitaria, Granada

# MAY

| | 19 |
| | 20 |
| | 21 |
| | 22 |
| | 23 |
| | 24 |

SCULPTOR
Giovanni Boccaccio. *Le livre des cleres et nobles femmes*.
MS. Fr. 599, f. 58
French, fifteenth century
Bibliothèque Nationale, Paris

# MAY

| 25 | |
|----|---|
| 26 | |
| 27 | |
| 28 | |
| 29 | |
| 30 | |
| 31 | |

DAIRY SCENE
*The da Costa Hours*. M. 399, f. 5v
Flemish. c. 1515
The Pierpont Morgan Library, New York

# JUNE

| | 1 |
| | 2 |
| | 3 |
| | 4 |
| | 5 |
| | 6 |

HAYING. June
Pol de Limbourg. *Les tres riches heures du duc de Berry.*
MS. 65/1284, f. 6v
French, fifteenth century
Musée Condé, Chantilly (Ph: Giraudon/Art Resource)

# JUNE

| 7 | |
| 8 | |
| 9 | |
| 10 | |
| 11 | |
| 12 | |

FEEDING CHICKENS
*Tacuinum Sanitatis*. MS. s.n. 2644, f. 65r
Italian, c. 1385
Österreichische Nationalbibliothek, Vienna

Ol lan de nře ſeiġné
nul cent quatre binġ
et ſept ou mois
daouſt acoucha la roẏne de fra̋

# JUNE

| | 13 |
| | 14 |
| | 15 |
| | 16 |
| | 17 |
| | 18 |

ATTENDING A BIRTH
Jacques de Guise. *Histoires des nobles princes de Hainaut*.
MS. 149, tome 3, f. 119. French, fifteenth century
Bibliothèque Municipale, Boulogne/s/Mer
(Ph: Giraudon/Art Resource)

Qui petit ascir et qui quiert inuenit petenti aduir et pussani aictur

Ulee niuenciou

# JUNE

| | 19 |
| | 20 |
| | 21 |
| | 22 |
| | 23 |
| | 24 |

MINER
Montferrant. *Les douze dames de rhétorique.* MS. Fr. 1174, f. 29r
French, fifteenth century
Bibliothèque Nationale, Paris

# JUNE

25

26

27

28

29

30

LAY ARTIST PAINTING THE MADONNA AND CHILD
Giovanni Boccaccio. *Le livre des femmes nobles et renommées*.
MS. Fr. 598, f. 86
French, fifteenth century
Bibliothèque Nationale, Paris

# JULY

| | 1 |
|---|---|
| | 2 |
| | 3 |
| | 4 |
| | 5 |
| | 6 |

COLLECTING COCOONS AND BREEDING
SILKWORMS
Giovanni Boccaccio. *Le livre des femmes nobles et renommées*.
MS. Fr. 598, f. 68v
French, fifteenth century
Bibliothèque Nationale, Paris

# JULY

| 7 | |
| 8 | |
| 9 | |
| 10 | |
| 11 | |
| 12 | |

WOMAN SURGEON PERFORMING CAESAREAN SECTION
Jean Bondol. *Histoire ancienne jusqu'a Cesar.*
vol. 2, f. 199 (detail)
French, c. 1375
H. P. Kraus Rare Books and Manuscripts, New York

# JULY

| | 13 |
| | 14 |
| | 15 |
| | 16 |
| | 17 |
| | 18 |

CHRISTINE DE PISAN, WRITING
*Collected Works of Christine de Pisan.* MS. Harley 4431, f. 4
French, fifteenth century
British Library, London

# JULY

19

20

21

22

23

24

MASONS CONSTRUCTING THE CITY WALL (detail)
*Collected Works of Christine de Pisan: Cité des Dames.*
MS. Harley 4431, f. 290
French, fifteenth century
British Library, London

# JULY

| 25 |
|----|
| 26 |
| 27 |
| 28 |
| 29 |
| 30 |
| 31 |

DRAWING VINEGAR FROM A KEG
*Tacuinum Sanitatis.* M. s.n. 2644, f. 85v.
Italian, c. 1385
Österreichische Nationalbibliothek, Vienna

# AUGUST

|  | 1 |
|--|---|
|  | 2 |
|  | 3 |
|  | 4 |
|  | 5 |
|  | 6 |

COLLECTING COCOONS AND WEAVING SILK
Giovanni Boccaccio. *De claris mulieribus.*
MS. Royal 16 Gv, f. 54v
French, fifteenth century
British Library, London

# AUGUST

| | 7 |
| | 8 |
| | 9 |
| | 10 |
| | 11 |
| | 12 |

FRYING BREADS
Dioscorides. *Tractabus de herbis*. MS. Lat. 993, f. 142r
French, fifteenth century
Biblioteca Estense, Modena (Ph: Giraudon/Art Resource)

# AUGUST

| 13 | |
|----|--|

| 14 | |
|----|--|

| 15 | |
|----|--|

| 16 | |
|----|--|

| 17 | |
|----|--|

| 18 | |
|----|--|

MILKING A COW
*Bestiary.* MS. Bodley 764, f. 41v
English, c. 1225-1250
Bodleian Library, Oxford

# AUGUST

| | 19 |
| | 20 |
| | 21 |
| | 22 |
| | 23 |
| | 24 |

SELLING LEEKS
*Tacuinum Sanitatis*. MS. s.n. 2644, f. 25
Italian, c. 1385
Österreichische Nationalbibliothek, Vienna

# AUGUST

| 25 | |
| 26 | |
| 27 | |
| 28 | |
| 29 | |
| 30 | |
| 31 | |

ARTIST WITH MALE APPRENTICE
Giovanni Boccaccio. *Le livre des cleres et nobles femmes*.
MS. Fr. 12420, f. 86
French, fifteenth century
Bibliothèque Nationale, Paris

# SEPTEMBER

|   | 1 |
|---|---|
|   | 2 |
|   | 3 |
|   | 4 |
|   | 5 |
|   | 6 |

SPINNING WITH A DISTAFF
Giovanni Boccaccio. *Le livre des cleres et nobles femmes*.
MS. Fr. 599, f. 40
French, fifteenth century
Bibliothèque Nationale, Paris

# SEPTEMBER

| | |
|---|---|
| | 7 |
| | 8 |
| | 9 |
| | 10 |
| | 11 |
| | 12 |

WOMAN TEACHING
Giovanni Boccaccio. *Le livre des femmes nobles et renommées*.
MS. Fr. 598, f. 71v
French, fifteenth century
Bibliothèque Nationale, Paris

# SEPTEMBER

| | |
|---|---|
| 13 | |
| 14 | |
| 15 | |
| 16 | |
| 17 | |
| 18 | |

LAY SISTER PREPARING MEDICATIONS (detail)
J. du Ries. *Quart volume de histoire scolastique.*
MS. Royal 15 Di, f. 18
Flemish, 1470
British Library, London

# SEPTEMBER

| | 19 |
|---|---|
| | 20 |
| | 21 |
| | 22 |
| | 23 |
| | 24 |

SELLING FISH
*Tacuinum Sanitatis*. MS. s.n. 2644, f. 82v.
Italian, c. 1385
Österreichische Nationalbibliothek, Vienna

# SEPTEMBER

25

26

27

28

29

30

PLAYING A DULCIMER
Giovanni Boccaccio. *Le livre des cleres et nobles femmes*.
MS. Fr. 599, f. 29
French, fifteenth century
Bibliothèque Nationale, Paris

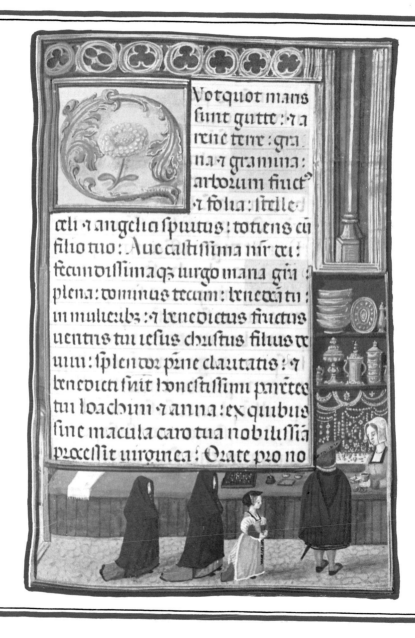

Votquot maris
sunt gutte : 7 a
rene tene : gra
na 7 gramina :
arborum fructꝰ
7 folia : stelle
celi 7 angelici spiritus : totiens cū
filio tuo : Aue castissima uirgo tci :
fecundissimaqꝫ uirgo maria gra
plena : dominus tecum : benedca tu :
in mulieribꝰ : 7 benedictus fructus
uentris tui iesus christus filius te
uuu : splendor pure claritatis : 7
benedicti sunt honestissimi parētes
tui ioachim 7 anna : ex quibus
sine macula caro tua nobilissiā
processit uirginea : Orate pro no

# OCTOBER

1

2

3

4

5

6

WOMAN SELLING IN A SHOP
*Hours of the Virgin*
Flemish, c. 1525
Collection The Viscount Astor, Oxford

# OCTOBER

| | 7 |
|---|---|
| | 8 |
| | 9 |
| | 10 |
| | 11 |
| | 12 |

TRANSPORTING SALT
Jean Cuba. *Le jardin de santé.* Vol. II. "Le sel"
French, c. 1501
Petit Palais, Paris (Ph: Bulloz)

# OCTOBER

|  | 13 |
|---|---|
|  | 14 |
|  | 15 |
|  | 16 |
|  | 17 |
|  | 18 |

MAKING A BED
Guillaume de Digulleville. *Pélerinage de la vie humaine.*
MS. 1130, f. 83
French, fourteenth century
Bibliothèque Sainte-Geneviève, Paris

# OCTOBER

| 19 | |
| 20 | |
| 21 | |
| 22 | |
| 23 | |
| 24 | |

PREPARING AND CUTTING LINEN
*Tacuinum Sanitatis*. MS. s.n. 2644, f. 105v
Italian, c. 1385
Österreichische Nationalbibliothek, Vienna

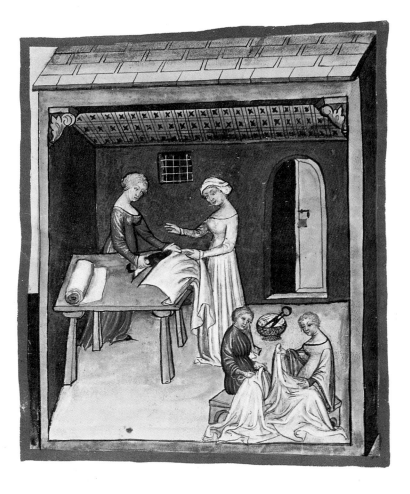

# OCTOBER

|  | 25 |
|---|---|
|  | 26 |
|  | 27 |
|  | 28 |
|  | 29 |
|  | 30 |
|  | 31 |

PICKING CABBAGES
Thomas de Cantimpré. *De natura rerum . . . tacuinum sanitatis*. Codex C-67, f. 104v
Italian School, early fifteenth century
Biblioteca Universitaria, Granada

KL Nouember habet dies. xxx.
Luna vero. xxix.

      d  Festum omniū sanctorum

xiii  e  Commemoratio defunctoꝝ

ii  f  Hilarionis episcopi

      g  Vitalis & Agricolæ

x  A  Zachariæ pꝭs Ioannis. B.

      b  Leonardi confessoris

xviii  c  Prosdocimi episcopi

vii  d  Coronati martyris

      e  Dedicatio basilicæ saluatoris

xv  f  Tryphonis cum. 7. filiis

# NOVEMBER

| | 1 |
| | 2 |
| | 3 |
| | 4 |
| | 5 |
| | 6 |

BREAKING FLAX FOR LINEN
*Heures de la Bienheureuse Vierge Marie.* November.
Dutuit B. 37, f. 15r
French, early sixteenth century
Petit Palais, Paris (Ph: Bulloz)

# NOVEMBER

| | 7 |
| | 8 |
| | 9 |
| | 10 |
| | 11 |
| | 12 |

WOMAN AT FORGE
Guillaume de Lorris and Jean de Meun.
*Le Roman de la Rose.* MS. 1126, f. 115
French, fourteenth century
Bibliothèque Sainte-Geneviève, Paris

# NOVEMBER

13

14

15

16

17

18

ARTIST PAINTING SELF-PORTRAIT ON PANEL
Giovanni Boccaccio. *Le livre des femmes nobles et renommées*.
MS. Fr. 598, f. 100v
French, fifteenth century
Bibliothèque Nationale, Paris

# NOVEMBER

19

20

21

22

23

24

NUNS TREATING PATIENTS IN A HOSPITAL
*Livre de la vie active des religieuses de l'Hotel-Dieu*
French, fifteenth century
Musée de l'Assistance Publique, Paris

# NOVEMBER

| 25 | |
|----|---|
| 26 | |
| 27 | |
| 28 | |
| 29 | |
| 30 | |

PREPARING NOODLES
*Tacuinum Sanitatis.* MS. s.n. 2644, f. 45v
Italian, c. 1385
Österreichische Nationalbibliothek, Vienna

Paguenes lassiatieque fut fille de colopho= mus plebeieque et rural. Elle fut plaine desprit : Car elle fuyoit oieusete et touf= iours faisoit qlq chose. Elle trouua liuention de tam= dre la laine : et de filler au rouet .

et de faire nouuel= les brodures et tapisseries. Sa renommee fut si grãd quelle tomba iucques a dire que mineruc ne auoit riens mineute et que tout venoit delle. Les poetes

# DECEMBER

|   |   |
|---|---|
|   | **1** |
|   | **2** |
|   | **3** |
|   | **4** |
|   | **5** |
|   | **6** |

SPINNING
Antoine Dufour. *La vie des femmes célèbres.*
MS. 17
French, c. 1505
Musée Dobrée, Nantes (Ph: Giraudon/Art Resource)

# DECEMBER

| | 7 |
|---|---|
| | 8 |
| | 9 |
| | 10 |
| | 11 |
| | 12 |

WEAVING TAPESTRY
Christine de Pisan. *Cité des dames*. MS. ADD. 20698, f. 90
Dutch version, 1475
British Library, London

# DECEMBER

|  | 13 |
|  | 14 |
|  | 15 |
|  | 16 |
|  | 17 |
|  | 18 |

FARM CHORES. December
*The Golf Book of Hours*
MS. ADD. 24098, f. 29v
Flemish, c. 1500
British Library, London  (Ph: E.T. Archive)

# DECEMBER

| | 19 |
| 20 |
| 21 |
| 22 |
| 23 |
| 24 |

WOMAN APOTHECARY PREPARING MEDICINE
IN PHARMACY
*Tacuinum Sanitatis.* MS. s.n. 2644, f. 53v.
Italian, c. 1385
Österreichische Nationalbibliothek, Vienna

# DECEMBER

| | 25 |
| | 26 |
| | 27 |
| | 28 |
| | 29 |
| | 30 |
| | 31 |

WAITING ON TABLE
*The da Costa Hours*. MS. 399, f. 2v
Flemish, c. 1515
The Pierpont Morgan Library, New York

# SELECTED BIBLIOGRAPHY

Adams, Carol; Bartley, Paula; Bourdillon, Hilary; Loxton, Cathy. *From Workshop to Warfare: The Lives of Medieval Women.* Cambridge: Cambridge University Press, 1983.

Bell, Susan Groag. "Medieval Women Book Owners: Arbiters of Lay Piety and Ambassadors of Culture." *Signs* (Summer 1982): 742–768.

Bogin, Meg. *The Women Troubadours.* New York: Paddington Press Ltd., Two Continents Publishing Group, 1976.

Crump, C. G., and Jacob, E. F. *The Legacy of the Middle Ages.* Oxford: Oxford University Press, 1962.

Egbert, Virginia Wylie. *The Medieval Artist at Work.* Princeton, N.J.: Princeton University Press, 1967.

Ehrenreich, Barbara, and English, Deirdre. *Witches, Midwives and Nurses, A History of Women Healers.* Old Westbury, N.Y.: The Feminist Press, 1973.

Heer, Friedrich. *The Medieval World.* New York and Scarborough, Ontario: New American Library, 1961.

Hollister, C. Warren. *Medieval Europe. A Short History.* New York: John Wiley & Sons, 1982.

Hughes, Muriel Joy. *Women Healers in Medieval Life and Literature.* New York: King's Crown Press, 1943.

Kelly, Joan. "Early Feminism and the Querelle des Femmes." *Signs* (Autumn 1982): 4–28.

Lone, E. Miriam. "Some Bookwomen of the Fifteenth Century." *Colophon* (September 1932): 83–90.

Mitchell, Sabrina. *Medieval Manuscript Painting.* New York: The Viking Press, 1965.

O'Sullivan, Jeremiah, and Burns, John F. *Medieval Europe.* New York: F. S. Crofts & Co., 1946.

Pizan, Christine de. *The Book of the City of Ladies.* Translated by Earl Jeffrey Richards. New York: Persea Books, 1982.

Power, Eileen. *Medieval Women,* edited by M. M. Postan. Cambridge: Cambridge University Press, 1975.

*The Secular Spirit: Life and Art at the End of the Middle Ages.* Introduction by Timothy B. Husband and Jane Hayward. New York: E. P. Dutton & Co., in association with The Metropolitan Museum of Art, 1975.

Tuchman, Barbara W. *A Distant Mirror: The Calamitous 14th Century.* New York: Alfred A. Knopf, 1978.

Willard, Charity Cannon. *Christine de Pizan: Her Life and Works.* New York: Persea Books, 1984.

# PICTURE CREDITS FOR DETAILS

Page 1: MS. Fr. 599, f. 50, Bibliothèque Nationale, Paris

Opposite title page: MS. 71, f. 18, Musée Condé, Chantilly (Ph. Lauros-Giraudon/ Art Resource)

Dedication page: MS. C.A. 14, f. 47r, Biblioteca Nazionale, Naples (Ph: Scala/ Art Resource)

Introduction: MS. 76/1362, f. 10v, Musée Condé, Chantilly (Ph. Lauros-Giraudon/Art Resource); MS. C.A. 14, f. 47r, Biblioteca Nazionale, Naples (Ph: Scala/Art Resource); Playfair Books of Hours, November, Victoria & Albert Museum, London (Ph: E.T. Archive); MS. ADD. 20698, f. 17, British Library, London

Jan. 13: MS. 134, August, Bibliothèque, Angers (Ph: Lauros-Giraudon/Art Resource)

Feb. 25: MS. Arsenal 5070, f. 188, Bibliothèque Nationale, Paris

May 13: MS. Arsenal 5073, f. 336, Bibliothèque Nationale, Paris

July 1: MS. Fr. 12311, f. 187v, Bibliothèque Nationale, Paris

Sept. 1: MS. Fr. 599, f. 48r, Bibliothèque Nationale, Paris

Sept. 25: MS. Fr. 599, f. 19, Bibliothèque Nationale, Paris

Oct. 13: MS. Arsenal 5070, f. 51v, Bibliothèque Nationale, Paris

Nov. 7: MS. Fr. 1537, f. 44, Bibliothèque Nationale, Paris

Picture credits page: MS. Fr. 598, f. 31, Bibliothèque Nationale, Paris

Colophon page: MS. 229, f. 329r, Beinecke Library, Yale University, New Haven

NOTE: The photographs for the *Tacuinum Sanitatis*, MS s.n. 2644 in the collection of the Österreichische Nationalbibliothek in Vienna, and the *De natura rerum . . . tacuinum sanitatis*, Codex C-67 in the Biblioteca Universitaria, Granada, were made from facsimiles in the collection of The Historical Library, Yale Medical Library, New Haven.

Designed by Clifford Selbert
Production coordination by Nancy Robins
Composition in Garamond by
Monotype Composition Company, Inc.
Separations by Dai Nippon Printing Company Ltd.
Printing and binding by Artes Gráficas Toledo, S.A.